V

LIFE
MOTIVATORS

Published by RDO
6 Cotswold Business Village
Moreton-in-Marsh
Gloucestershire
GL56 0JQ
United Kingdom

*A catalogue record for this book is available
from the British Library.*

Designed by
the workshop, Longhope,
Gloucestershire

Printed by
Regent Publishing Services,
Hong Kong

ISBN: 1-903680-02-6

It's your desire not your ability that will determine your success.

*A wish
changes nothing —
a decision
changes everything.*

A WISE PERSON
learns by the experience of others.

AN ORDINARY PERSON
learns by his or her own experience.

A FOOL
learns by nobody's experience.

People may doubt what you say, but they will always believe what you do.

*It does
not matter
what anybody
says, thinks or does;*

**it's what *YOU* do
that really matters.**

A joy that is shared
is a joy that is *doubled*.

A worry that is shared
is a worry that is *halved*.

HOT HEADS AND COLD HEARTS NEVER SOLVED ANYTHING.

*Exercise
does not take
time out of
your life;
it will put
life into your time.*

If you do the things you need to do when you need to do them, then some day you can do the things you want to do when you want to do them.

The oldest,
shortest words
'**YES**'
and
'**NO**'
are those that
require the
most thought.

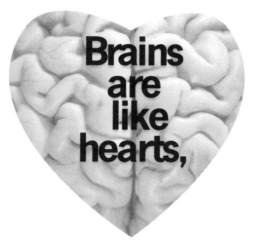

Brains are like hearts,

THEY GO WHERE THEY ARE APPRECIATED.

A SINGLE REASON WHY YOU <u>CAN</u> DO SOMETHING IS WORTH A HUNDRED REASONS WHY YOU <u>CAN'T</u>.

If you weather the storm you'll reach the port.

If you continue to live in the past your life is history and you are missing the joys of today and tomorrow.

Cancel the
membership
to the
'If I'da club' and
the *'If Only club'*
and join the *'I Am Club'*,
and the *'I Can Club'*.

SUCCESS IS NOT

GETTING ON TOP

BUT HOW YOU

BOUNCE

ON THE BOTTOM

THAT COUNTS.

PEOPLE WHO WAIT
FOR SOMETHING
TO TURN UP
MIGHT START
WITH THEIR OWN
SHIRT SLEEVES.

Your greatest asset is your brain- your greatest resource is time.

The people you mix with are like the buttons on an elevator, - they will either take you up or take you down.

Some of the happiest people in the world

appear to be those who do the most for others.

Instead of:

You win some and you lose some,-

how about

you win some and you learn some.

The only place where **money** /'mʌni/ n

comes before **work¹** /wɜːk/ n

is in the dictionary.

Many people concentrate on finding fault; it is as though there must be a reward for criticising.

Probably the greatest
way of keeping
a conversation lively
and interesting
is the greatest question
ever asked -

'why?'

All you have to do
to change your life
is to change your attitude.
It really is that simple,
but it isn't always easy.

All you have to do
to stop feeling BAD
is to start feeling GOOD.
It really is that simple,
but it isn't always easy.

IF YOU ARE GOING TO THINK YOU MIGHT AS WELL THINK **BIG** – IT TAKES NO MORE CALORIES.

A friend by your side can keep you warmer than the most expensive coat.

If you were
going on holiday tomorrow,
what would you be doing today

?

So, don't procrastinate,
DO IT
NOW!

You cannot fail at anything until you actually **give up.**

One of the great ways to conquer fear is to keep doing the things you fear to do.

Worry never paid a bill

Worry never calmed a fear

Worry never cooked a meal

Worry never fixed a wheel

In fact, worry has

never done anything

One
guaranteed way
to make yourself
happy
is to make
someone *else*
happy.

'I must do something'
will always
solve more
problems than
**'something
must be done'.**

THE ERROR OF THE PAST IS THE WISDOM AND SUCCESS OF THE FUTURE.

One sure way
to get rid of a problem
is to stop calling it a problem
and call it a situation.

Very rarely is a person ruined by excessive praise, but almost certainly once every minute someone dies inside for lack of it.

GO ON - DO IT NOW!

A clever person turns great troubles into little ones and little ones into none at all.

The wise
judge by
what they **see**,
the foolish
by what they **hear**

ASK YOURSELF TODAY —
IS WHAT I'M DOING
NOW
HELPING ME TO
GET CLOSER
TO MY GOALS?

You can't manage time. You can't get more minutes in an hour. You can manage you and how you use those minutes & hours.

We have
50,000
thoughts per day,

so can you imagine
what you would achieve
if that 50,000 were all positive?

Sticks and stones may break my bones, but words can never hurt me.

Be wiser than other people if you can,

BUT DO NOT TELL THEM SO.

Love
is true

**when you don't see eye to eye,
but can still walk hand in hand.**

*If you think
education is expensive,
then wait
till you see
what ignorance
costs you.*

To avoid:

Resentment of another's success

Criticism of a neighbour's weaknesses

Impatience with youth's immaturity

Remorse over yesterday's failure

Wear a smile
and have friends.

Wear a scowl
and have wrinkles.

Commitment
is doing what you said
you would do
long after the feeling
you had when saying it
has passed.

To avoid:

Anxiety over today's problems
Worry over tomorrow's uncertainty
Waste of the moment's opportunity
Procrastination with one's present duty

Doing
nothing

is the most tiresome job in the world,
because you can't stop and rest.

*It's not so much
what you say
as the **manner**
in which you say it.
It's not so much
the language you use
as the **tone**
in which you convey it.*

OTHERS HAVE HAD TO FACE
GREAT DISCOURAGEMENT
AND GREAT OBSTACLES
AND HAVE OVERCOME THEM

AND WHAT OTHERS
HAVE DONE,
SURELY YOU CAN TOO.

Don't be unhappy if some of your dreams don't come true—

be thankful your nightmares don't.

We are not judged
by the number of times
we fail but by
the number of times we
succeed

&the number of times
you succeed can be in that
proportion to the number
of times you fail.

It's your choice

Choose to love rather than hate

Choose to smile rather than frown

Choose to build rather than destroy.

It's your choice

Choose to persevere rather than quit

Choose to praise rather than gossip

Choose to heal rather than wound.

It's your choice

Choose to give rather than grasp

Choose to act rather than delay

Choose to forgive rather than curse.

The distinguishing line between success and failure can be stated in 5 words -

I did not have time.

THREE TIPS TO SUCCESS:

Have a five year plan for success

Realise that you not others ultimately control your success

Brainstorm alternatives to tough decisions

THREE TIPS
TO SUCCESS:

Celebrate your achievements

Shrug off your setbacks

Develop a support network

It is amazing that otherwise intelligent people don't realise that if you treat people badly it will eventually come back to them.

Don't communicate merely to be understood, communicate so tha you cannot possibly be misunderstood.

NEVER ASK A QUESTION YOU DON'T WANT TO HEAR THE ANSWER TO.

LAUGHTER IS A GREAT MEDICINE AND A SENSE OF HUMOUR REDUCES PEOPLE AND PROBLEMS TO THEIR PROPER PROPORTIONS.

There is no future living in the past.

Some people make the future, most people wait for the future to come to them.

A sense of humour
is not the ability to tell
jokes or be funny,
but rather the ability
to laugh at jokes
and notice what is funny.

Your potential is like a thought that hasn't come to your mind yet.

If you actually don't start out
the day with a smile,
it's never too late
to start practising
for tomorrow.

We learn
& remember

10% of what we **hear**

15% of what we **see**

20% of what we **see & hear**

40% of what we **discuss** with others

80% of what we **experience** directly

90% of what we **teach** others

THE GREATEST OF ALL FAULTS IS TO BE CONSCIOUS OF NONE.

PRAY *for the things you want,*

WORK *for the things you need.*

FEAR *is an imagination- not a reality. It's only the thought of what might happen that creates the fear.*

Fear holds us back
and prevents us from
acting appropriately in life
When we can actually
confront our fears
we see that they have
no reality.

Failure is not a person- it's an event.

Everything in life
is created twice -
once
in your mind
and
once
in reality.

ANGER,
is it worth it:

Do I really want to feel angry?
Will it change anything?
Is it worth giving up my peace of mind for?

It is
pretty
difficult
to keep
your mind
& your mouth

O open

at the
same time.

**TWO MEN
LOOKING
THROUGH
PRISON
BARS,
ONE
SAW MUD,
THE OTHER
SAW STARS.**

NO

Never take NO for an answer,

you can do anything

if you are willing to ask –

it takes ordinary people

to do ordinary things.

To handle a worry, ask yourself what's the worse thing that can happen, then imagine and visualise it in detail. Now plan a contingency and forget about the worry.

Love

has the power to

dissolve any

negative

experience

no matter what it is.

Generosity is the fastest way to open the heart. It connects us to the very heart of creation which is always giving. Think of ways to give and the whole experience of life will begin to change.

It
is
better
to light
a candle
than
curse
the
dark.

*When a person blames another
and points a finger at them,
remember there are three fingers
pointing at the one with the finger
pointing in the opposite direction.*

If you feel
ANGER,
HATRED
OR JEALOUSY
you are in self-destruct mode,
so decide to move out or stay in.

The only way
to live happily
with people *is to overlook
their faults
and admire
their virtues.*

Be careful
of the words
you speak,
make them soft
and sweet,
you never know from
day to day
the one's
you'll have to eat.

A thought on love.

*Love
is an
unusual game,
there are either
two winners
or none at all.*

It's better to forgive & forget than to resent & remember.

and modern ar̲ ̲ ̲ ̲ ̲de mopolitan ̲ ̲itional ̲ ̲
the backdrop to the friendly verge in a delightful diversity.

Researchers have apparently discovered that it is impossible to develop eye strain from looking on the bright side of things.

ful energy. Medieval, Georgian bustling port where the cos-
and modern architecture provide mopolitan and traditi̲ ̲ ̲ ̲ ̲on-

No one can help everybody, but everybody can help somebody.

It's more fun
and more
financially successful
when you
stop trying to get
what you want
and start helping
other people
to get
what they want.

OBSTACLES ARE THOSE FRIGHTFUL THINGS YOU SEE WHEN YOU TAKE YOUR EYES OFF THE GOAL.

A smile cannot be bought, begged, borrowed or stolen, for it is no earthly good to anybody until it is given away.

SUCCESS
*can be when you
get what you want.*

HAPPINESS
*is when you
want what you get.*

Isn't it funny how our days are identical suitcases, all the same size, but some people can pack more into them than others.

IT'S A MARK
OF A SUPERIOR
MIND TO BE ABLE
TO DISAGREE
WITHOUT BEING
DISAGREEABLE.

THE SAFEST WAY TO GET THE BEST OF AN ARGUMENT IS TO AVOID IT.

Show respect for the other person's opinion;

after all it's only an opinion and it is theirs.

We very rarely regret the things we have done. *We are much more likely to regret the things we haven't done.*

WHEN THE GOING GETS TOUGH THE TOUGH GET GOING.

Make promises **sparingly** *and keep them* **faithfully,** *no matter what it costs.*

Some people are like wheelbarrows: they don't go anywhere unless they are pushed

GREAT LITTLE SELF-MOTIVATORS:

Say

I am happy

I am feeling great

I am successful

ANOTHER GREAT LITTLE SELF-MOTIVATION

Say

*I am
financially secure*

I am feeling well

I am confident

DELETE THE NEGATIVE AFFIRMATIONS:

Don't ever Say:

I'm feeling terrible

I feel ill

I can't

DELETE THE NEGATIVE VISUALISATION:

Don't ever Say:

I'm sure I've got something
wrong with me

I'm just not clever enough

I don't have what it takes

I'm sure today is going
to be a bad day

YOU KNOW THAT EXCUSES ARE JUST EXCUSES:

Don't ever Say:

I'm too young

I'm too old

I'm never in the right place
at the right time

I'm just not lucky

I never went to the right school

If only I were healthier

Be cheerful, don't burden or depress those around you by dwelling on your aches and pains and small disappointments.

A little flattery will support a person through great fatigue.

A good rule
for going through life
is to keep the **heart**
a little softer
than the **head**.

What
the mind
of man
can accurately **conceive**
and **believe,**
it is forced to **achieve**.

Cheerfulness

IS THE ATMOSPHERE
UNDER WHICH
ALL THINGS THRIVE.

BETTER THAN
BEING THE HEAD
OF THE FAMILY
IS BEING
THE HEART
OF IT.

It's better
to live *one day*
as a lion
than *100 years*
as a sheep.

A HOUSE IS NO HOME UNLESS IT CONTAINS FOOD FOR THE SOUL AS WELL AS THE BODY.

We may give without loving, but we cannot love without giving.

A day of worry
is more exhausting
than a week
of work.

If
you are
willing to
admit
when
you are
wrong,
you are right.

AN APOLOGY IS A GOOD WAY TO HAVE THE LAST WORD.

**Take care
of the minutes
and the hours and minutes
will take care
of themselves.**

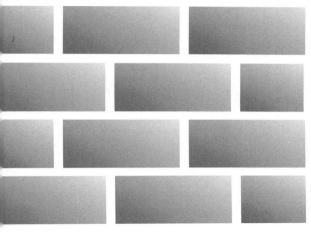

**YOU CANNOT BUILD
A REPUTATION
ON THE THINGS
YOU ARE GOING TO DO.**

*Books, Audio Tapes and Videos on
Sales, Leadership, Management, Customer Care
and Personal Development.*

Visit our website: **www.denny.co.uk**
Email: **success@denny.co.uk**
Telephone: +44 (0) **1608 651597**
Fax: + 44 (0) **1608 651638**

Mail: **RDO**
6 Cotswold Business Village
Moreton-in-Marsh
Gloucestershire
GL56 0JQ
United Kingdom

Visit the website for special offers:
www.denny.co.uk